Nature's Children

CATS

by Maggie da Silva

 Grolier Educational

FACTS IN BRIEF

Classification of cats

Class: *Mammalia* (mammals)
Order: *Carnivora* (carnivores)
Family: *Felidae* (cat family)
Genus: *Felis* (common cat)
Species: *Felis domestica* (domestic cat)

World distribution. As pets, throughout the world.

Habitat. In the wild, everywhere but Australia and Antarctica. Indoors as house pets; often allowed to wander outdoors.

Distinctive physical characteristics. Strong muscles and flexible spine give them great agility for jumping, balancing, and fitting through tight spaces. Special layer in the eyes (tapetum lucidum) helps them see in the dark. Ears can turn separately to hear sounds coming from different directions. Whiskers on face and front legs help to sense movements.

Habits. Strong hunting instinct; groom themselves often each day.

Diet. Carnivores, eating mostly chicken, birds, rodents, beef, and fish.

Library of Congress Cataloging-in-Publication Data

Da Silva, Maggie, 1964-
    Cats / Maggie da Silva
        p.   cm. — (Nature's children)
    Includes index.
    Summary: Describes the physical characteristics, behavior, distribution, and care of various types of domestic cats.
    ISBN 0-7172-9067-0 (hardbound)
    1. Cats—Juvenile literature. [1. Cats.]   I. Title.
II. Series.
SF445.7.D3   1997
599.75—dc21

97-5979
CIP
AC

This library reinforced edition was published in 1997 exclusively by:

 Grolier Educational
Sherman Turnpike, Danbury, Connecticut 06816

Set ISBN 0-7172-7661-9
Cats ISBN 0-7172-9067-0

Contents

Graceful and mysterious, independent yet affectionate, cats have fascinated people for centuries. First as hunters and later as friendly companions, cats have won the hearts of millions and millions of people.

There are many reasons why cats have become such popular pets. First of all, they are inexpensive to keep and beautiful to look at. They also are extremely clean animals. On top of this, having a cat as a pet can have wonderful health benefits. Studies have shown that people who have and care for pets are more relaxed and feel less lonely. This is especially true for senior citizens, for whom gentle, easy-to-care-for cats are an almost ideal pet.

Cats weren't always pets, however. At one time all cats were wild. In fact, common house cats are probably descended from the African wildcat, a small, striped cat that resembles the familiar tabby cat of today.

Today's cat lovers are very attached to their pets. And although cats may seem independent, they are really very attached to "their people" and rely on them for affection and understanding. It is no wonder that more than thirty million Americans share their homes with felines.

With their grace and mystery, cats have fascinated— and served—people for thousands of years.

The Hunting Instinct

Every cat, from the fiercest lion to the tiniest kitten, has a strong hunting instinct. (An instinct is a type of behavior that is part of an animal's basic nature.) Cats are born with a desire to hunt, and many of the games kittens play are really preparing them to become successful hunters. Batting a ball around the house, swiping at a dangling toy, or pouncing on a spool of thread or yarn are all ways for kittens to master the art of the hunt.

Some kittens grow up to become "professional" hunters. These cats earn their keep by catching mice and other pests for their human owners.

Long ago cats' hunting instinct insured them a steady supply of food. In contrast, most of the world's cats today get their food from human owners. Still, even the most pampered house cat—no matter how well it is fed—will spend part of its day hunting or trying to hunt. That is simply because modern-day house cats have the same instincts as their wild ancestors.

Even an insect can bring out a cat's hunting instincts.

Some Egyptian History

How long have people kept cats as pets? No one can tell for sure, of course. But archaeologists (people who study how humans lived long ago) have found ancient Egyptian records showing that domesticated, or tamed, cats date back at least 3,500 years.

Egyptians may have been the first group of people to take cats into their homes. But this did not happen overnight. About 6,000 years ago people in ancient Egypt had a terrible problem keeping mice and rats away from their stores of grain.

One day the Egyptians accidentally discovered that little wildcats were hunting and catching the pesky rodents for them. The grateful Egyptians welcomed the useful animals into their homes. These African wildcats gradually adapted to life with people and, in time, became domesticated.

The ancient Egyptians pampered and protected their cats far beyond what most cat owners do today. In fact the ancient Egyptians considered cats sacred, like their gods and goddesses. If a cat died accidentally, its Egyptian family would shave off their eyebrows as a sign of grief. And the punishment for killing a cat was death!

Curiosity—and their hunting instinct—can lead cats to strange places.

The Working Cat

Since they first protected Egyptian grain from rodents, cats have continued to serve as "professional" mousers. Even today, most ships keep a cat on board to protect the food stored below. And no barn is complete without at least one cat to keep mice out of the grain and hay. Stores and shops keep cats as well, using them to keep rats away from valuable merchandise. Home-owners, too, often see cats as a valuable tool for keeping away pests. This is as true for city dwellers as for people who live in the country or suburbs.

For professional cats mousing is both business and pleasure. Often a cat will play "Cat and Mouse" with a stunned mouse before killing it. In the same way cats frequently present their "catch" to their owners as a sign of affection and triumph.

Cats stalk their prey as they hunt.

Built for Speed

Powerful legs, feet, and claws give cats remarkable speed. The average house cat can reach 30 miles (48 kilometers) an hour in short bursts and can also jump up to five times its height.

Cats also have great physical agility. Flexible spines enable them to twist and turn in midair and "melt" through tiny spaces. Their strong leg muscles propel them to jump incredible heights! Cats also have an outstanding sense of balance and can walk on something as narrow as a pole or rope.

Occasionally a cat does fall from its perch. But the amazing animal can turn itself around and land on its feet. Its elastic muscles and flexible skeleton are able to absorb the impact of almost any fall. Maybe this is why cats have been said to have nine lives!

Cats love to leap and jump.

The Sensitive Cat

Cats have extraordinary senses. They can see, hear, and sense movements around them much better than their human owners. Cats' eyes have a special layer called tapetum lucidum that reflects light and helps them see in the dark. This is also why cats' eyes often seem to glow in the dark.

Cats can turn each of their ears separately to catch every noise. Because of this cats hear a much wider range of sounds than humans do, especially ultrasounds (high sound frequencies), which people cannot hear at all.

A cat can detect odors in two ways: with its nose and with a special part of its mouth called the Jacobson's organ. This keen sense of smell helps cats identify other animals.

Sensitive whiskers (called vibrissae) are located on the cat's face as well as in the area behind its front legs. These whiskers help the cat judge space. Whiskers can actually sense air movements. A cat can feel air moving around objects, so it can avoid them without even looking. A cat's senses are so sharp that it almost seems equipped with radar!

Cats are always on the lookout for something to hunt.

Indoor Cats . . . Outdoor Cats

Cats can live indoors, outdoors, or both! Outdoor cats are often less affectionate toward humans than indoor cats. These independent outdoor cats are used to "roughing it" outdoors. But they still need a warm place to sleep and should be let indoors when the weather is bad.

Many indoor cats live in houses and city apartments and rarely or never go outside. Their owners enjoy the companionship but may not appreciate some of their pet's instinctual habits, like scratching.

Both indoor and outdoor cats need to be fed every day. They need to be given fresh water as well. And all cats—regardless of where they live—should be given shots to protect them from rabies.

Sometimes a cat will be abandoned or lost and will go back to living in the wild. Then the cat is said to be feral. Feral cats are not tame, like outdoor cats. They may even be ill or dangerous. A feral cat should be reported to an animal shelter so trained professionals can try to catch it and give it vaccinations and care.

Most cats enjoy getting out in the fresh air.

Purebred Cats

Purebred cats are those whose ancestors were all of the same type. Although purebred cats are expensive, some people want them because they like the looks and character of a certain breed or because they want animals that can participate in shows and competitions.

Some purebreds are admired for their personalities as well as their looks. Two breeds known for having a sweet temperament are the Persian, with its long, silky fur, and the rare Abyssinian, with its smooth, unusual coat and large, intelligent-looking eyes.

The sleek, shorthaired Burmese has a playful personality and makes a great pet for families with children. On the other hand, the exotic-looking Siamese is perfect for someone who is a good listener. Siamese like to talk!

Some breeds are admired primarily for their looks. The tailless Manx is a popular breed. And few cat lovers can resist a sweet-faced Rex, with its large, pointy ears.

Whether purebreds compete at shows or not, these "aristocats" always receive plenty of well-deserved attention.

Mixed Breeds

Most cats are mongrels (their ancestors are of different, mixed breeds), and most mongrel cats are shorthaired "alley" cats. Coming in just about every size, color, and marking imaginable, these are the cats most people have as pets. They are also the cats we occasionally see wandering wild in fields or on city streets.

Although certain cat breeds are considered especially intelligent, cat owners quickly learn that there are smart cats and not-so-smart cats among every breed, including mongrels. A cat's behavior depends a lot more on the kind of treatment and attention the animal receives than on its genetic makeup, the hereditary characteristics that have been passed down from its parents.

A cat's stare can fascinate its owners.

Choosing a Cat

An animal shelter, such as the American Society for the Prevention of Cruelty to Animals (ASPCA), is one of the best places to adopt a cat. Generally shelters have many cats to choose from. Just as important, these cats usually are spayed, which means they have had surgery to prevent them from having kittens. They often have been vaccinated against certain diseases as well.

There are several things to look for when choosing a cat. The health of the animal is the most important point. A healthy cat is lively and playful, with bright, clear eyes. It also has a clean, glossy coat with no bare or thin patches. Its ears should be clean, inside and out.

Another important thing is the cat's personality. Some people want an affectionate "lap cat." Others want a more independent animal.

It sometimes takes a person a long time to decide on the right cat. But in some cases it is the cat who decides—by walking right up to the person or communicating affection in some way.

When a cat and a person like each other right away, they are sure to develop a close friendship over time. And no matter which cat a person chooses, the animal will always be grateful for a caring owner and a nice, cozy home.

Eating Habits and Food

House cats are carnivores (meat eaters), just like their wild cousins, lions and tigers. But even cats that hunt regularly cannot live on their prey. In fact, cats—even professional "mousers"—rarely eat what they kill.

For the most part house cats live on a diet of canned cat food, which contains meat, fish, or chicken, along with some added calcium. This gives cats the basic nutrients they need for a long, healthy life.

In addition to a balanced diet cats should have a bowl of fresh water available to them at all times. And cats, like people, have individual tastes in food. There are cats that like an occasional hard-boiled egg . . . or even a stalk of steamed broccoli!

Although dog food is good for dogs, it should never be given to cats. Most dog food contains preservatives that are actually poisonous for cats.

Cats usually are willing to share with one another—even when it comes to food.

Grooming

Cats are very particular about their hygiene, and they clean themselves several times a day, using their tongues, teeth, and paws. Unlike dogs, cats should never be bathed, even if they look dirty. Cats hate water baths, which are also bad for a cat's sensitive skin. If a cat seems dirty for a long period of time, it is probably in bad health, and a veterinarian should be called.

Most cats seem to enjoy having their fur brushed. This type of grooming is also a chance for owners to check their pets for pests such as fleas or ticks. Shorthaired cats need only an occasional brushing to get rid of loose hair and to keep their skin healthy. Longhaired cats, however, need to be gently brushed every day to keep their fur clean and tangle-free.

As part of general grooming, owners should also provide cats with a scratching board or post of some kind. This will help cats keep their front claws worn down to the proper length. It is also important for owners to think carefully before having their pets declawed. A cat without its front claws is nearly defenseless outdoors—it will even have difficulty climbing a tree to escape from another animal.

Cats clean and groom themselves several times each day.

A nice stretch makes a cat feel good—and ready for action.

How to Handle a Cat

The correct way to pick up a cat is to put one hand under its front legs and then, with the other hand, scoop up its bottom. Cats should never be grasped around the middle, held by the tail, or picked up by the scruff of the neck. Such mishandling is uncomfortable for the cat and can even cause injury.

Proper handling is safe and comfortable for both the person and the animal. It is very important for owners to be considerate of their pets and to make an effort to handle them correctly and gently. Considerate owners are rewarded with the affection and trust of their pets.

Cat Behavior

Listening to the soft purr of a contented cat is one of the pleasures of cat ownership. Kittens start purring when they are about a week old. For them it is a way to let their mothers know that they are getting enough milk. Experts say the mysterious purr happens when blood vibrates in a vein in the cat's chest.

Cats communicate in ways other than purring. A roll on the back says, "I trust you." And when a cat rubs its face on someone, it means, "You belong to me."

Cats sleep for about 16 hours a day. In their waking hours they may roam around or spend a long period of time watching a faucet drip. They may even pass a whole afternoon stalking shadows. Lying in the sun seems to satisfy cats as much as it does humans.

Cats just love to lie in the sun.

The Territorial Cat

Cats are territorial, but the amount of territory each cat considers its own varies. Indoor cats probably consider the entire house or apartment to be theirs and theirs alone. (Although they seem willing to share it with their human roommates.)

A cat marks the boundaries of its territory by scratching things. This leaves behind a visual mark as well as some of the cat's scent, which comes from the animal's paw pads. Male cats also stake their claim by spraying an area with urine.

A male cat in the country may have a territory of 100 acres (40.5 hectares) or more. Females tend to stick closer to home, within 15 acres (6 hectares) or so. A cat tours its territory frequently to check on its scent posts and to see if any other cats have strayed into its area. Both male and female cats will defend their territories and chase a trespassing (unwelcome) cat away.

Cats often strike mysterious poses.

Training

One reason many people find it easier to own a cat than a dog has to do with training. Dogs require all sorts of training. They need to be "house trained" and have to learn to go to the "bathroom" outside. They also need to learn certain commands, such as "Sit," "Stay," and "Come." Similarly, dogs are taught to walk "at heel" on a leash. And most dogs are taught at least a few tricks, if for no other reason than to amuse their owners.

But cats, unlike dogs, rarely perform tricks or walk on a leash. In fact, cats need very little training at all. Kittens can be quickly trained to use a litterbox, and as long as the box is scooped out regularly, the cat will carefully use the litterbox whenever it needs to.

Occasionally, though, a cat will have a bad habit. It may, for example, scratch floors or rip furniture with its claws. Usually this is because it does not understand the "house rules." Then gentle instruction may be necessary to keep pets from scratching things or climbing on kitchen counters.

It takes only a little time to teach a kitten to use a litter box.

Catnip

Catnip (*Nepeta cataria*) is a leafy herb that can have a powerful effect on some cats, making them especially playful, energetic, or sleepy. Different cats respond differently to catnip, and some cats don't react to it at all.

Many cat owners buy their pets toys stuffed with catnip. People who live in the country may grow a patch of catnip near the house for their cats' pleasure.

Many cats like to chew catnip and roll around in catnip leaves. After eating a little catnip, a cat may race through the house or fall asleep in a strange position. Catnip is too strong for kittens, and even adult cats should only be given a small amount. A little bit of catnip goes a long way!

It doesn't take much to make a toy for a playful, lively kitten.

Trimming a cat's claws protects both people and furniture.

Cats and Other Animals

Cats are hierarchical animals, which means that they like to know who is "top cat." Most cats are loners, preferring their own company to that of anyone else, even another cat. Some cats can become friends, but most keep a respectful distance from each other.

When two cats do meet, they immediately establish which cat is dominant. The more aggressive cat (the one that is more quick to attack) will threaten the other by approaching sideways, with an arched back. The less aggressive cat will crouch defensively. Then the less aggressive cat will run away.

Most cats will also run away when they meet a big animal, such as a dog. But when a cat decides to stand its ground, the dog often will back down. Most dogs will not risk a scratch on the nose or worse.

Cats and dogs, however, can learn to live peacefully in the same house, especially if they are introduced to each other when they are young. People can help their animals get along by teaching their dogs respect for felines. And cats need to be taught to tolerate the clumsy affection of dogs, who sometimes try to lick them off their feet!

Health Care

Cats are hardy animals, but sometimes they do get sick. When a cat is ill, it may seem tired and without appetite. Sick cats sometimes drink a lot of water, or they vomit or have diarrhea. A runny nose or a dirty, dull coat are other signs that a cat may be sick.

Most cats recover from an illness after a day or two. But if a cat doesn't get better by itself, a veterinarian should be consulted.

People can help their cats stay healthy by making sure their pets get all the shots, or vaccinations, they need. Keeping pets free of common pests such as fleas, ticks, ear mites, and intestinal worms is also important. A vet can provide medicine and advice for pest-free cat care.

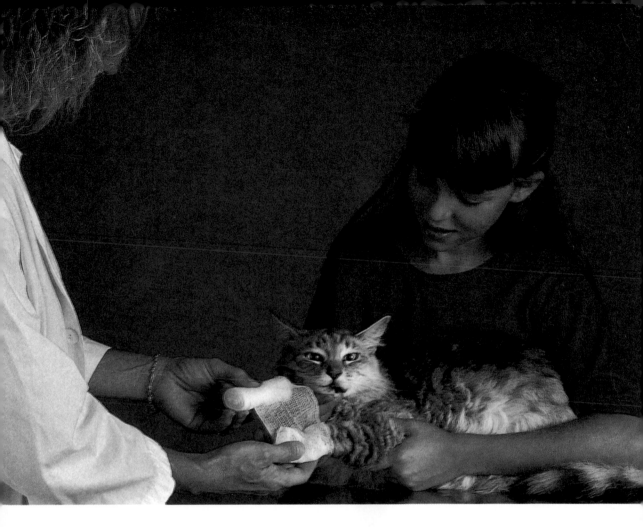

*A vet can help with everything from a runny
nose to an injured paw.*

"Free Kittens to Good Home"

A female cat can mate two or three times a year. During these times she is said to be "in heat." If she is let outdoors, she will likely find a mate and become pregnant. Every cat needs a home, and while purebred kittens are easy to give away, mongrels are not.

That is why many cat owners choose to spay, or neuter, their pets. When cats are spayed or neutered they can no longer produce kittens. This involves a small operation that is usually done at an animal shelter or in a vet's office. Cats recover from this operation quite quickly.

Neutering has additional advantages, as well. Neutered male cats are less territorial and less aggressive. Neutering a male can also help stop undesirable behavior such as spraying urine inside the house.

Every cat needs a good home, regardless of whether it is a purebred or not.

Giving Birth

A female cat is pregnant for about nine weeks. As the cat's time grows near, owners can prepare a soft, warm place for their cats to give birth. But the cat has the final say in this matter and may choose the back of a closet instead.

Cats like to be alone when they give birth and often do it in the middle of the night. The birth process may take a long time, depending on the number of kittens. Although four kittens is common, there can be as many as eight in a litter!

After each tiny kitten is born, the mother licks it clean. Although the kitten's eyes are still closed, it uses its sense of touch and smell to start nursing on its mother's milk.

It can be tempting to touch the tiny newborn kittens. But newborns—and their mother—should be left strictly alone so they can get to know each other.

Kittens!

After a few days it is all right to touch the kittens. Stroking a young kitten very gently helps it get used to people. After about two weeks kittens can be held for a few minutes every day.

Kittens grow fast! They are curious, intelligent animals. A four-week-old kitten is ready to explore its surroundings, looking for objects to investigate and play with. Play is a very important activity that helps kittens develop coordination and good reflexes.

After about six weeks the kittens can be weaned, slowly taking them away from their mother's milk and putting them on a diet of solid food. At eight or nine weeks they are ready to go to homes of their own. The kittens should not be taken from their mother any earlier than this, and not all of them should be removed at once. One kitten should stay with the mother cat until it is at least 10 weeks old, to keep her company.

Giving a Kitten a New Home

A kitten's first night in a new home can be a frightening experience. The tiny creature is used to being with its mother and brothers and sisters. Being alone in a strange place can unnerve even the most ferocious kitten.

To make the animal feel more comfortable and secure, owners should keep the new kitten in a small, warm room, like a bathroom, instead of letting it roam around. A hot water bottle wrapped in a towel can be tucked into its bed, with a ticking clock nearby. This reminds the kitten of its mother's warm body and heartbeat. After a few days the kitten will feel right at home!

*Moving to a new home can be a frightening
and lonely experience.*

Shows and Cat Clubs

Cat shows are popular among people with purebred cats. There purebred cats compete against others of the same breed for prizes based on their looks and how well they conform to certain standards of size, color, shape, and other qualities.

There are 25 cat breeds that are recognized by the Cat Fanciers Association, the largest cat club in the United States. But not all breeds are represented at every show.

Going to a cat show can be a lot of fun. People can see their favorite breeds, from Siamese to Persian. There are also very rare and exotic cats, from breeds that have almost no fur to cats that like to swim! And most of all, cat shows are great places to see and enjoy the wonderful world of felines.

Words to Know

Agility.   The ability to move easily, quickly, and gracefully.

Aggressive.   Likely to attack or try to dominate.

Archaeologists.   People who study ancient human life by examining remains such as tools, pottery, buildings, fossils, and artifacts.

Calcium.   A mineral that helps strengthen bones in animals.

Elastic.   Able to stretch, expand, or bend.

Feline.   A cat.

Feral.   Wild; an animal that has gone back to the wild.

Hereditary.   Traits or characteristics passed down from the parents to the child.

Hygiene.   The practice of keeping oneself clean and healthy.

Mouser.   A cat that regularly hunts for mice and rats.

Spayed.   Neutered; operated on in order to prevent the birth of kittens.

Ultrasound.   Vibrations that are just like sound with frequencies above the range of human hearing.

Vaccinate.   To give a disease-preventing medicine.

Wean.   To get a child or mammal used to food other than its mother's milk.

INDEX

Cover Photo: Martin Harvey (The Wildlife Collection)
Photo Credits: Norvia Behling (Behling & Johnson Photography), pages 4, 7-8, 13-14, 22,
25-26, 31, 33, 35-36, 39, 41, 45; John Giustina (The Wildlife Collection), page 17; Martin Harvey
(The Wildlife Collection), page 20; Lynn M. Stone, pages 11, 29.